How to Start Your Podcast

The Ultimate Beginner's guide to podcasting and useful tips about equipment, launch, self-marketing and podcast's quality improvements

By

Marvin Dale

© Copyright 2020 by (Marvin Dale) - All rights reserved.

This document is geared towards providing exact and reliable information in regards to the topic and issue covered. The publication is sold with the idea that the publisher is not required to render accounting, officially permitted, or otherwise, qualified services. If advice is necessary, legal or professional, a practiced individual in the profession should be ordered.

- From a Declaration of Principles which was accepted and approved equally by a Committee of the American Bar Association and a Committee of Publishers and Associations.

In no way, it is legal to reproduce, duplicate, or transmit any part of this document in either electronic means or in printed format. Recording of this publication is strictly prohibited and any storage of this document is not allowed unless with written permission from the publisher. All rights reserved.

The information provided herein is stated to be truthful and consistent, in that any liability, in terms of inattention or otherwise, by any usage or abuse of any policies, processes, or directions contained within is the solitary and utter responsibility of the recipient reader. Under no circumstances will any legal responsibility or blame be held against the publisher for any reparation, damages, or monetary loss due to the information herein, either directly or indirectly.

Respective authors own all copyrights not held by the publisher.

The information herein is offered for informational purposes solely, and is universal as so. The presentation of the information is without contract or any type of guarantee assurance.

The trademarks that are used are without any consent, and the publication of the trademark is without permission or backing by the trademark owner.

All trademarks and brands within this book are for clarifying purposes only and are the owned by the owners themselves, not affiliated with this document.

Table of contents

INTRODUCTION 6

CHAPTER 1: GETTING STARTED WITH A PODCAST 8

1.1 What is a Podcast? 9

1.2 Things to Consider while choosing a Podcast Topic 12

1.3 Types of Podcasts 15

1.4 Things to be discussed in a Podcast 19

1.5 How Long And Frequent Should Your Podcast Episode Be? 23

CHAPTER 2: EQUIPMENT REQUIRED AND ORGANIZATION OF EPISODES 25

2.1 Podcast Workflow and Content Strategy? 26

2.2 Use of Content calendar to produce better Podcasts 30

2.3 Podcast Equipment's needed for beginners 33

2.4 Podcast Equipment for Advance Users 35

CHAPTER 3: TIPS FOR PODCAST RECORDING AND EDITING 40

3.1 Podcast Recording tips 41

3.2 Podcast Mixing Tips 46

3.3 Equipment Required to Edit Podcast 52

3.4 Ways to Edit Podcast 54

CHAPTER 4: MARKETING OF A PODCAST 59

4.1 How to Launch and monetize podcast? 60

4.2 Strategies to Promote your Podcast 69

CONCLUSION 74

REFERENCES .... ERROR! BOOKMARK NOT DEFINED.

Introduction

Several people listen to podcasts more than at any time before. According to Thomas Edison, in the past four years, the number of Americans listening to a podcast each week has grown by 120 percent, and every month 90 million Americans listen to a podcast. As a business person, learning to start a podcast is something you must find helping when you reach at level to expand audience and develop your business by selling content. As the podcast's audience continues to expand, there's never been a better time for your company, brand, or personal hobby to start a podcast. Podcasts are a perfect way to create a real public link. Podcasts allow you to engage your audience with exclusive long-form material, instead of the broken link you create via social media. Podcasts are more comfortable than posts of blogs; people can hear to podcasts during working out, driving, or doing house chores. Podcasts are as diverse as the people that make them. Pop culture, psychology, history, and even a fantasy city where aliens are buddies of the Yeti are great podcasts. The only obstacle to producing a podcast is your creativity. There is substantial unexplored space in the podcasting industry. Apple Podcasts include at least 600 million forums, 23 million YouTube channels but just 800,000 podcasts. You do not need to be a technical guy, nor do you need any money to learn how to do a podcast. If you know the importance of producing content for your company and brand (e.g., blogging), you know the importance of podcasting. You can reach a brand new audience by making a podcast: people who would otherwise never discover your lengthy content because they prefer the audio content. You don't have to be a proven creator of the material or have a blog to be a good podcaster. A podcast is best way to create an audience from place yourself as an expert within your industry.

Furthermore, podcasts also give the potential for getting traffic on websites. All podcast directories provide a link to your website, and you can guide listeners to your web page at the end of each broadcast, as it is your podcast. Podcasting audiences increased dramatically after 2018. According to the 2019 Edison Research Podcast User Survey, 51% of Americans of 12 + age listened to a podcast, with 32% listening in a month, and 22% listening in a week. There are several divisions and subdivisions available on Apple Podcasts where listeners get new content. Which means the material on the podcast will be highly focused. You can seek out people who have interest in your topic. Podcasts had a diverse audience in 2015, with listeners between the ages of 18 and 44 being male and female adults alike.

Nonetheless, the 2019 data from Edison reveals that in recent years, podcast listeners have skewed a little more male and a little bit older (35–54 years old). Finally, starting a podcast lets you position yourself as an expert on your subject. It helps build your market, and it also makes it easier to sell your product or service because you are the source of reputation. Being viewed as an expert will help to persuade potential customers to purchase your goods.

Chapter 1: Getting Started with a Podcast

Podcasts are now deeply defined parts of pop culture, and you are sure to have a favorite (or seven) that will help make your travel more sustainable. Every broadcaster who has a voice recorder app is keen to get into the game, it's not as easy as it may seem to create a professional-sounding podcast. It's essential to know that podcasts demands a real struggle to get started before you jump into anything. They aren't mere recordings of talking people (not the good ones, anyway). Pat Flynn, the Smart Passive Income podcast host, advises that you approach podcasting in the same way as you would handle any other major project. Podcasting is incredibly fun and thrilling, but one thing you need to do before starting podcasting is committing. You have to concentrate to podcasting completely, because you have to do everything that is functionally beneficial. This process would take time and effort. It's tempting to believe podcasts are easy to make because they're just audio, but don't get tricked. They can consume a huge time, particularly at first, to put together. Also, podcasts do well when regularly published. If you're interested in building a fan base of some sort, you must be ready to film episodes automatically. Podcasting can all be enjoyable work, but it's always working and should be regarded as such. Nor would you hope to get rich from podcasting. It's possible to arrange revenue from podcasting, but that typically includes promotions and financing — both of which you will get after you have made a listenership that's efficient enough to make advertisers worthwhile. If you are not interested in initiating a podcast for fun or conveying your voice, you may not get a lot out of it.

1.1 What is a Podcast?

The emerging technology has led to various development items being introduced in enterprises. With various aspects of business transforming daily with changing customer requirements and market demands, these tools have become necessities for staying afloat in this highly competitive marketplace. Over the years, podcasting has gained immense popularity. Nowadays, companies increasingly use podcasts to boost their prospects. It is a potent resource for marketing. On mobiles, computers, podcasts are the new talk radio. The increased use of mobile phones has led to explosive growth in podcasting.

A podcast is an arrangement of episodes comprising of spoken word digital audio files that a user can download for easy listening in to a personal device. Once they are uploaded, a user can subscribe to the podcast to receive the digital files. Applications involving podcasting and streaming services provide a convenient, integrated way to manage a queue for personal consumption across numerous podcast sources and playback devices.

In October 2000, Tristan Louis defined the idea of combining and adding audio and video files to RSS feed in a draft. Dave Winer, a computer programmer and an author of the RSS format, put the idea into practice. Once an obscure method of distributing audio material, podcasting has become a known medium for the dissemination of audio content, whether for personal or corporate use. Podcasts are precisely the same as radio shows, but they do exist as audio files that can be played at the convenience of a listener, anytime, or anywhere. The first application made it feasible for this method was iPodderX, created by August Trometer and Ray Slakinski.

By 2007, audio podcasts did what was done previously by radio broadcasts, which had been the basis of TV talk shows and news programs since the 1930s. This change came about due to internet technologies' evolution coupled with expanded user exposure to cheaper audio recording and editing hardware and software. Matt Schichter launched his weekly talk show, The BackStage Pass, in October 2003. Live recording of the hour-long radio broadcast, transcoded to 16kbit / s audio for web streaming dial-ups. Despite the lack of a commonly accepted identification name for the medium at the time of its production, it is widely believed that The Backstage Pass that became known as Matt Schichter Interviews was the first podcast to be published online. Adam Curry began his show Daily Source Code in August 2004. It was a show that focused on chronicling his daily life, providing news, and discussions about podcasting growth, as well as supporting new and emerging podcasts. Curry published it as an effort to gain interest in improving what would become known as podcasting and as a mode of checking the program outside of a laboratory environment.

The name of the podcast, the Daily Source Code, was chosen to attract an audience with a technological interest. Daily Source Code started at a grassroots manufacturing level and was initially aimed at podcast developers. These developers were encouraged to build and produce their projects when their audience became interested in the format, and as a result, they developed the code used to make podcasts. As more people discovered how easy it was to create podcasts, there rapidly emerged a group of pioneer podcasters. Apple released iTunes 4.9 in June 2005. These iTunes added formal support for podcasts which neglected the idea to use a separate program for transferring and downloading to a mobile device. While this has made access to podcasts more convenient and widespread, independent developers have also effectively ended the advancement of podcatchers. Besides, Apple issued cease and desist orders to many podcast application developers and service providers to use the words "iPod" or "Pod" in their products. The logo used by Apple in its iTunes applications to reflect podcasting. Many podcasts from public radio networks such as the BBC, CBC Radio One, NPR, and Public Radio International have placed many of their radio shows on the iTunes platform within a year. Major local radio stations, including New York City's WNYC and Philadelphia's WHYY-FM radio, and Los Angeles' KCRW posted their programs on their websites, and also on, the iTunes platform.

Today most podcasts are audio-only, although there are video podcasts. Podcasting also evolved out of a need for material in the context. That means something that entertains, teaches, or encourages you when other activities are dull or rote. Many podcasts will be dedicated to one particular subject. In each episode, the hosts will discuss that topic. It's very personal sometimes, like dog training, and sometimes it's more common, like how to live a happier life. Then, every episode of that podcast will address something different within that subject – nutrition tips for competing in a triathlon race. Every episode is typically presented by some regular presenters, which talk about the particular subject. Many podcasts are simple like a conversation among friends about something they're all excited about, like movies or running a business. But some are genuinely polished and super-professional, including music themes, sound effects, professional editing, and more.

One of the most usual places people listen in, for example, is in the car. Of course, you can't watch the video there, so audio content is fantastic. Similarly, podcasts are pleasant to listen to in the gym when you're mowing the grass or on the drive to work. Any time that's wasted can be an audio moment. That means you need to listen to something, of course, so you may need to get a set of headphones to connect to your smartphone. A podcast series usually covers one or more reappearing hosts engaged in a discussion about a particular topic or current affair. Within a podcast, review, and content can go from scripted to improvise. Podcasts combine intricate and imaginative development of sound with thematic topics ranging from science analysis to journalism in the slice of life. A lot of podcast series provide links, guest biographies, transcripts, extra resources, commentaries, and even a community forum to discuss the content of the show. We are no strangers to the overloading of information. Audio details that attempt to engage customers can be a welcome break from the monotony, with the Internet being filled with a large amount of written content.

Additionally, it leaves enough space for the speaker to express the message in a highly immersive way that does not merely have written content. A survey of 300,000 podcast listeners found that 63 percent of the respondents had purchased what the host had been promoting. This suggests podcasts can be used to engage the audience and positively influence their purchasing decisions. There are plenty of reasons people are inspired to make a podcast. The podcast producer, who is also the podcast host, may wish to increase professional exposure, build a group of like-minded listeners or bring forward pedagogical or political ideas (possibly under philanthropic support). Since podcast material is often free or, at least, accessible to the average user of podcasting, podcasting is often regarded as a disruptive medium, averse to sustaining conventional revenue models. Long-running podcasts with an extensive back catalog are vulnerable to binge consumption.

1.2 Things to Consider while choosing a Podcast Topic

Often, there is incorrect arrangement between the companies that produce content and the markets that the digital marketer seeks to attract. Individuals can frequently assume the audience or construct material holding "personas" that are not based on real evidence but have been made up in a conference room instead. For podcasting, the stakes are much higher, because you're committing to a series of episodes, created at regular intervals, and you're setting listener expectations from the first podcast on what you're going to cover, what's your style, how long each episode will be, etc. In other words, choose the wrong topic, and you are stuck with it for a while. Even if that topic does little for your business, also if the audience that your podcast attracts never spends money on you or recommends you to others. If you feel indifferent or cynical about the subject, you must now cover that subject in episode after episode. In short, it's not as easy to choose an issue as you would suppose.

A good podcast should address the audience's needs: a difficulty or issue to be solved, a question they need to answer, or a subject they want to learn more about. What effect would you like to address your audience? What kind of problem do they want to resolve and they are looking for you? That could be an inspiration. It could be understanding. It could be education, training, and less seriousness to be taken into things. It could be a lot of stuff. In the abstract, what question are you trying to solve is the bird's eye level? That may be the problem you're trying to address in your business in a lot of other ways, but now this podcast is how you're manifesting. Of course, you must first know who your audience is to understand what your audience wants. Researching your audience is a first step essential for producing any form of related content (including podcasts). If you can manage to conduct primary research with a research firm, that is the gold standard.

Still, even if you cannot engage a research firm, you can do surveys or focus groups, asks your salesman regarding the type of questions prospects and clients request. You can review any feedback you get through customer service centers. There are a lot ways to get to know your audience better. Observation is another technique. Watch how your client moves through your store. Check web analytics and heatmaps to see how they perform online while browsing your website. There are lots of windows in your audience's hearts and minds, so take a look. Also, you could mine the abundant data on social media.

By studying social media analytics, the Conversation Research Institute, founded by Jason Falls, has gained completely unexpected insights into the public of a business. You could discover, for example, that your customers are more involved in fashion than the general public, which might push you to introduce new colors or designs for your goods (even though you're selling scooters or laptops). If you're a veterinarian, you wouldn't be podcasting about your services and fees. It would be dull in the first place. And, second, that would interest very few people. When you want to meet your market, look at what they need more generally, and add on top of what you need (which is more patients). A veterinarian who specializes in show-dog care could create a podcast focused on showing animal preventive healthcare, which could include diet and exercise advice, how to keep a shiny coat, and what kinds of typical complaints can be prevented and how, and so on. When an urgent health problem for their show dog occurs, you can bet listeners will be ready to call this veterinarian (at least if they're driving distance away).

Check out some other podcasts before you can figure out what's going to make your podcast unique. The perfect manner to find out what makes a worth podcast while is to subscribe to a couple of feeds that pique your curiosity. Listen for a couple of weeks to these feeds (provided they're weekly) and find out what you like and don't like about them. You might find your angle from the notes that you're taking. Note that downloading and listening to other podcasts should be educational and constructive, not a fodder raid for your show. Do not steal content, special effects, or unique segments from another podcast. Approach the podcasts of others just like you would visit somebody's website for the sake of understanding. Being inspired is all right; just don't make your podcast a carbon copy of your inspiration's work. Avoid criticism of another podcast on your own when you have your podcast up. Criticizing the work of someone else is no way of improving yours. It is better to show support overall for other podcasts and the podcasting community than to insult or trash the hard work of others.

Whether you've decided to go into religion, music, or technology, the perfect way to make your podcast distinct is to find an angle you're comfortable with (Polka: Misunderstood Music, Sports History's Great Travesties, Science Fiction's Forgotten Grands). There might be the possibility that your first show may impress such a unique additional angle that you will need to start another podcast specifically to target that audience. Do not apologize for being "another podcast on" or point out what you do wrong in comparison with others. What makes a podcast fun is the passion and confidence that you exude when the mics are hot. Address your subject with authority and energy, and enjoy the recording of your time. If you make a podcast with a blast, your audience and you will enjoy it. That confidence could even inspire others to put themselves on the podcast.

1.3 Types of Podcasts

Hearing various types of podcasts can be a way to engage in a storytelling form that lets you just sit back and listen. It can be a nice break from looking at a screen or a book's pages, and it can also be a way for the podcast host to take you to another location, if only for an hour or two. Podcasts are on the rise, with a 23 percent increase in the number of podcast listeners per year. To put it the other way, the large number of podcast listeners jumped from 13 million to almost 21 million from

2016 to 2019, and those numbers are only expected to grow in the years to come. So, what makes a podcast reverberant with its listeners and keep them tuned week after week? It's a combination of podcast format and podcast host vocal qualities. Looking at the qualities of the most popular podcasts and their hosts can help you discover how to turn your podcast into a show that is widely listened to. Here are some of the various kinds of podcasts you can imitate. The top-rated podcasts available on iTunes and the podcast host's vocal qualities and styles make them so engaging and good interviewers.

1. Nonfiction Narrative Style of Storytelling

That's one of the most admired podcast formats, but mastering is tricky. This space is inclined towards the domination of journalists who are great at getting information from their subjects in-depth and insight. These podcasts retell others' true stories by using the interviewee's audio clips, as well as layer on their editorialization of the stories at hand.

The Style of Narration

The podcast host is Ira Glass (among many other traits), a writer, producer, reporter, and editor. His way of storytelling is one of an omniscient narrator — he seems to know everything about the role of characters in the story that they might not yet have come to grips with fully. He allows the characters' audio clips to speak for themselves, yet summarizes the characters' actions in a manner that helps bring the audiences deep within the character's motivations and hooks them.

Podcast Host Vocal Qualities

Ira has been a host of radio for many years. His voice is not the typical voice of radio announcers that you may expect to hear. He described his voice as a bit "nerdy" and "nasally," all of the qualities that make him appear more accessible. You feel like you hear a story from someone you know, not someone who might seem a little out of reach (like a booming voice on the radio would be). The fact that Ira sounds like the next-door-man helps attract listeners in.

2. Hybrid Mode

A hybrid podcast has a set host but often has hosts or speakers from other guests that contribute to the show. It usually begins with a host comment or monologue and then moves from another source into a panel discussion, interview, or contribution.

The Style of Narration

The style of narration differs, depending on the story that the author has chosen to read aloud, which is one of the captivating notions about this podcast. You do not know what genre, style, or author will crop up on the show, which is a great way to keep listeners tuned every week.

Podcast Host Vocal Qualities

One can describe the voice of Deborah Treisman as calming and soothing. Since the podcast aims to tell a story, her voice is setting the scene for a relaxed listening experience. She talks in an authoritative tone.

3. Interviews / Debate panel

Another popular podcast hosting style has one host throughout the show, with either a single guest interviewee or multiple guests. This type of podcast provides different viewpoints for listeners and is usually a popular format with political podcasts. Political Gabfest is a famous podcast that uses the format for the panel discussion.

The Style of Narration

The narrative style is more conversational. Even though the podcast is split into different segments, the discussion is much more like a conversation with your family members or friends. The link for the listener is that the format makes you feel like you hear in on a friends group and their thoughts on different political issues.

Podcast Hosts Vocal Qualities

Political Gabfest has three hosts. The initial host is John Dickerson, who usually reads intro and monolog on the start. Thanks to its commanding tone, his vocal style is similar to that of a radio announcer. Indeed, his voice makes him the perfect moderator of the panel discussion, and he can bring the conversation back to the original topic, if it starts drifting, throughout each show. The other two hosts have singular and peculiar voices that make them easily related and easy to hear.

4. Updated Content

Repurposing content is another popular way to pull your podcast together. The content available in 'repurposed style' podcasts usually ranges from workshops, interviews, seminars, and so on, and can serve to enhance listeners' experience. A famous example of a type of podcast using repurposed content is The Moth.

The Moth

Every week the podcast features the best stories from all over the United States that have been told on stage. The moth can assemble these stories because the own listeners of The Moth submit the accounts and audio files. Topics vary from personal and social experiences, as well as other histories of cultural relevance.

The Style of Narration

The narrator is also the audience-everybody who stands up on stage to tell their own unique story is a Moth listener. In this way, the podcast does a real job of creating human connections on the podcast between the listeners and the speakers. Such type of podcast is a different way for listeners to engage and hook on.

1.4 Things to be discussed in a Podcast

You may have been spending a lot of time brainstorming sections as a podcaster, which you can integrate into your podcast. Even if you have a particular podcast subject and a fixed format, a few segments will bring your podcast some variety and make it much more engaging. It can be challenging to brainstorm parts, though. You have heard people say you need a podcast. You just don't know where to start, though. You wonder what kind of podcast you want to create. During your episodes, you wonder what you're going to be talking about. You wonder how each chapter is formatted. All of this wondering doesn't necessarily cause things to get done. The critical part that makes finding the other puzzle pieces much easier is identifying what your series in your podcast show will revolve around.

1. Your Thoughts

You can create a whole podcast that revolves around your ideas. As long as your thoughts are captivating, people may decide to stick around when they watch some of the episodes on your podcast. Make sure that your dreams from each episode follow a common theme when creating a podcast show based upon your opinions. Do you talk politics all over? Are you just talking about animals? Make sure that your thoughts are on a common theme.

2: Expert Interview

One of the easiest ways to optimize your podcast is by using it to interact with other niche experts. Having an experienced person on your show means more exposure for that expert (the people in your audience see the podcast episode). You (the expert will share with their audience the podcast episode). If you bring hundreds of experts to their massive audiences to promote your podcast, we're talking about a significant stream of traffic. That considerable stream of traffic can potentially change life for your online credibility — which would skyrocket if you get well-known podcasting experts.

3: Blog Posts

If you feel uncomfortable talking off-the-cusp, you can start your podcast by reading your blog posts word-for-word, while making small tidbits available. While your podcast should have a better strategy for creating content in the long run, this is an excellent short-term strategy to win trust. When doing podcasts, you need to have confidence and comfort before you can go off-the-cusp with success. In the beginning, you could stumble. Stumbling is an uncomfortable but vital part of the process and is inevitable. Better now to stumble than later. Just get it away with it.

speakers. Such type of podcast is a different way for listeners to engage and hook on.

1.4 Things to be discussed in a Podcast

You may have been spending a lot of time brainstorming sections as a podcaster, which you can integrate into your podcast. Even if you have a particular podcast subject and a fixed format, a few segments will bring your podcast some variety and make it much more engaging. It can be challenging to brainstorm parts, though. You have heard people say you need a podcast. You just don't know where to start, though. You wonder what kind of podcast you want to create. During your episodes, you wonder what you're going to be talking about. You wonder how each chapter is formatted. All of this wondering doesn't necessarily cause things to get done. The critical part that makes finding the other puzzle pieces much easier is identifying what your series in your podcast show will revolve around.

1. Your Thoughts

You can create a whole podcast that revolves around your ideas. As long as your thoughts are captivating, people may decide to stick around when they watch some of the episodes on your podcast. Make sure that your dreams from each episode follow a common theme when creating a podcast show based upon your opinions. Do you talk politics all over? Are you just talking about animals? Make sure that your thoughts are on a common theme.

2: Expert Interview

One of the easiest ways to optimize your podcast is by using it to interact with other niche experts. Having an experienced person on your show means more exposure for that expert (the people in your audience see the podcast episode). You (the expert will share with their audience the podcast episode). If you bring hundreds of experts to their massive audiences to promote your podcast, we're talking about a significant stream of traffic. That considerable stream of traffic can potentially change life for your online credibility — which would skyrocket if you get well-known podcasting experts.

3: Blog Posts

If you feel uncomfortable talking off-the-cusp, you can start your podcast by reading your blog posts word-for-word, while making small tidbits available. While your podcast should have a better strategy for creating content in the long run, this is an excellent short-term strategy to win trust. When doing podcasts, you need to have confidence and comfort before you can go off-the-cusp with success. In the beginning, you could stumble. Stumbling is an uncomfortable but vital part of the process and is inevitable. Better now to stumble than later. Just get it away with it.

4: Talking about Something you Enjoy

Whatever you choose on your podcast to talk about, you've got to decide to talk about something you enjoy. If you're afraid to do your next podcast, don't be surprised if you don't take off your podcast. The most successful podcasters are the people in each of their episodes, who show passion for what they do. They provide a meaningful conversation that touches on some points most people skip over or even don't think about.

5: Frequently Asked Questions

Ask your followers on social media to submit questions, and randomly pick a couple to answer on your podcast.

6: Guest Player

Invite experts, colleagues, relatives, influencers, musicians, and other prominent people to your podcast. You can have a conversation with them, give a lecture to your audience, make them take charge of your podcast episode, do an interview, or have them co-host.

7: Recent News

Look up and think about the news about your podcast. Even if it's not explicitly connected, consider addressing it inside a section if you're interested in learning about the news.

8: Recommended

Offer your listeners artist, music, album, recycle, product, tool, book, game, video, destination, and other recommendations. Only let your listeners know what you are interested in at the moment!

9: Truth of the Day

Do you know, or have you learned an interesting fact recently that your listeners would be interested in? Tell the viewers!

10: Tale of the Day

Do you have a captivating story about your life, food, home, relationships, jobs, animals, etc.? Speak it to your audience!

11: Review / Comment

Review or recapture a song, album, case, book, game, series, or movie (concert, festival, award show, sporting event, etc.). Anything you have an interest in, and some information about, is important, consider reviewing it.

12: Minute on Social Media

Creating a hashtag and reading out messages using the hashtag. You will connect with your listeners on your podcast and let them contribute to a fun episode.

13: Quote of the day

If you've got a funny or motivational quote to share, on your podcast, they all make up a great episode.

14: Remarks

Feature an artist, a song, a video, a show, a place, a particular subject, or anything else you'd like to speak in depth. A spotlight is similar to a critique, except that spotlights are focused more on factual facts, and reviews are focused more on your opinions.

Even one or two creative segments can make your podcast considerably more engaging. Parts are a great way to break up your lengthy or burdensome content, so now and then it's a good idea to consider adding some segments. These are just a few ideas that offer a part you can customize for your podcast as an excellent basis. Please note, only pick sections that suit your podcast and that you think will appeal to your audience. Then, don't be afraid to extend and make these segments your own, the more you customize and own your parts, the more engaging they will be.

1.5 How Long And Frequent Should Your Podcast Episode Be?

Determining how frequently your podcast (their frequency) depends very much on your content. If you're talking about a weekly television show, then it's quite apparent you should have a weekly podcast. But did you consider an episode semi-weekly (two a week), too? Maybe an initial-reaction episode with reviews directly after the television show airs, and then a subsequent, more thought out event. Or perhaps you'd like to be amongst the first to talk about the latest tech news. You would then be expected to be every day. Many podcasts are bi-monthly, while others are monthly only. Subscribe to every Podcast weekly. Determine the timeliness of your content first, then set a schedule and try to stick to it. A weekly format seems to be the most common and consistently most comfortable to hold onto. After you have selected your duration, then you can choose the optimum length of your show.

Your frequency dramatically depends on the length of each episode. When you have an incredibly loyal audience, it seems overkill to release one-hour episodes every day (under the same podcast that is). If a customer goes on a one-week break, they must return to five hours of the content of that series, which can be quite challenging. But a monthly podcast on the opposite side should not automatically be a two- or four-hour show. When you record so much content, it's excellent, but split it up into smaller episodes to make it simpler for your listeners. The more frequently you update your website, the more you'll love Google, and the easier it can be to build a loyal audience.

Podcasts are a multi-tasking tool-that is, while you are doing something else, you can listen to a podcast. If you want to know the duration for a podcast, you may want to know how long "something else" is. US average commuting time, for example, is 26 min. If you're making a podcast longer than the average commute time, you might realistically expect that podcast to be less pleasing for those who listen to podcasts while traveling.

An average, which - by its very nature - means the commute of many peoples takes shorter, whereas others take longer. So, the data might be worth a look. The average total duration of a podcast in 2019 is about 37 minutes; the average length of a podcast in the category of video games is twice that. But that number of 37 minutes covers all podcasts, whether famous or not. How long does one get popular? The average duration of a top 100 podcast (in October 2018) is 53 minutes. It turns out. Megaphone, too, announced by July 2019 that podcasts were getting shorter.

Research in August 2019 found that the most common YouTube advertisements were just 6 seconds in duration. And in December 2019, RAIN News compared the total length of daily news podcasts with the number of ads they contained- and how long they had taken to get going. A Nigerian podcast survey at the end of 2019 reports that 54 percent of Nigerians recommend podcasts for shorter than 40 minutes (so nearly half prefer to be longer). So keep your podcasts short if you want to produce daily content. Maybe the average length of 10 to 15 minutes would be between. If you are looking at a weekly schedule, aim for a maximum of 60 minutes and up to 90 minutes of monthly podcasts. These are rough estimates, but if you stick to them carefully, you do not unnecessarily lose audiences.

Your podcast's length is a significant factor in its success. Determining the range is a complex equation of various variables that combine to give the audience an idea of what they want. Consider these elements when you sign your podcast to make sure it's one of the best on the market.

Chapter 2: Equipment Required and Organization of Episodes

With proper planning, an adequate podcast starts, even for the comedy "off-the-cuff." If you organize your material, while recording, you encourage yourself to be more creative. In reality, you promote more imagination and spontaneity. Most podcasters claim that preparing all of their material would take away the risk of events happening. Does the planning take the fun off your show? Not at all. You will spend more time worrying about making the next piece of content better and more surprising, while you spend less time trying to worry about the next part of the material. The secret to getting your content to become entertainment is to organize your content.

A show clock is one tool that most radio hosts use to organize their show. It is a rundown of what's going to happen on the show and when certain pieces of material happen. Once you have a co-host, the show clock becomes much more relevant. The clock is bringing all show participants on the same page. Each host knows what is going to happen, and when it will happen. For instance, the show will open first. It could be the theme recorded in 60-seconds. An introduction would accompany that in 4 minutes. This will include the content preview. This comes up in the show, along with guest detail. This way, as you complete the clock, you keep filling it out. Now that you've got the show schedule, you can use your brainpower to make every piece of content spectacular. Be imaginative. Be innovative.

Fill in the notes with descriptions and tales. Know just how you're going to make them fun. In there, get this call-to-action. Will episode will have a similar clock. Many begin with the theme of the show and its intro.

The watch lets you be imaginative. Most people decline to rehearse every aspect of their podcast because they fear it destroys any of the show's spontaneity. Only think of a speech you gave. When you've repeated the message a few times, anxiety sets in just before you go on stage.

On the other hand, when the speech has been rehearsed many, many times, you finally learn it by heart. The level of anxiety about delivering the content is not as high. You feel a lot more comfortable when you start. There's no question about making mistakes or missing pieces. You just relax. That is when it sets in on spontaneity. Spontaneity in your expression arises more when you're not thinking about presentation mechanics. Your mind can travel through the material, naturally. This helps you get very involved with the public and the staff. Once you hit this stage, fantastic, imaginative, spontaneous things happen. For your interview, the same can be said. Your podcast will be filled with many "oh wow" moments when you know the content, have established a precise aim for the series, and have planned out a strategy to achieve that aim. The clock of the show lets you rehearse and arrange the material before you hit the mark. It will make you feel relaxed and encourage you to be creative.

2.1 Podcast Workflow and Content Strategy?

Segment Strategy

It's essential to start with the end in mind for both new and current podcasts, explicitly about your audience, and the faith that the value proposition for your viewers and the reason you're doing a podcast is self-evident.

Segment Preparation

A lot of people just want to get going and have already hit the record button.

But when you've already had a dozen or so episodes under your belt, you'll find there's a lot involved in the preparation, especially if podcasting is anything even slightly on your horizon as a content strategy.

Segment Execution

There is a lot involved, and it can sound frightening. You will have to accept a great deal of ambiguity because it yields results for your show. And the complexity doesn't mean it can't automate, simplify or even outsource items. Both complexity and simplicity indeed coexist. It's the results that matter for us. Do you have a solo series or a series based on an interview? Have you got a Co-host? Has your podcast a theme in it? Would you want to try a different structure of an episode? Do you fear that your audience will get bored with our content? And if you're going to change? Or are you "podfading" and just plain tired and need a break?

This can all be tackled by grouping your podcast into different seasons. If you need a break, they encourage you to take a sabbatical from your show. They allow you to establish targeted themes for each season. You may turn the show style, including who is hosting, who is inviting, or whether it is a solo show. And all this without surprises for your listeners, as you announce the end of the current season or the start of the following seasons. Each season is a perfect excuse for a relaunch of the podcast and much needed promotional activities. If you're about to launch a podcast, take the time to go through the VPD process to get clarification and a product market appropriate for your show. If you have already started podcasting without any of this in mind, it's not too late to start and revisit now and then. If you have a season-based podcast, review your goals and value proposition for each season.

Now it's time to map out your podcast's most significant aspect, the content. Podcasts are no exception to the proverb "content is the king." Your podcast's standard will ultimately be decided by your topics, dialogue flow, personality, and overall engagement. It is a good idea to keep a list of the show topics going. Note it down as soon as an idea strikes, and plan it for a show to come. One way to come up with questions is to recognize when you are struggling for a presentation on a great subject. You are going to have a casual chat, talk shop about freelancing, and web design when all of a sudden, it's clear you have hit something exciting and relevant for the show. Write them down. Many podcasts split into segments every single episode. If your niche is somehow tied to the current events, covering news topics as part of your show may be a good idea. A guest interview is perhaps a significant component of your style. Plan for each of these segments, and consider the pacing and function of each section. Ultimately, talking about some kind of script for your series is advantageous. That is going to be diverse for everyone. The preference is to have a few sentences written in advance to be used at the beginning of the show, something to get it off to a strong start and introduce the subject and the guest better. The show's remaining topics are planned using short bullet lists to signify which points you want to focus on. The idea is to ensure that you cover what you want to cover while keeping the delivery natural and a little spontaneous. It is up to you, once again, to find the right balance.

Research all components of your podcast to provide your audience with the most relevant material. Your writing style should be conversational with a friendly language, restricting the use of jargon or industry-specific terms to please your listeners. The first segment will be the most interesting for holding the attention of listeners.

This section will be appealing to the public at large. Great content to support most is encouraged. News and current affairs related to the podcast theme are often of interest to a whole country. The subsequent reports can be more comprehensive and focus on particular areas of interest. Each section should be no more than 2-4 paragraphs, depending on the quality of the text.

In the podcast script intro, you can suggest introducing every episode of your podcast by this intro. Your listeners will listen to it a lot, so it is probably best to keep it short, maybe 10 or 15 seconds. With the +30 seconds skip setting on most podcast apps, the podcast intro won't be skipped over. What are you saying, then? Be sure to introduce the show host and its title. If you have any co-hosts, this is the right time to let your listeners know about them. Now is the time to give your viewers a glimpse of what they hope to hear on the show. For example, if you have something interesting and exciting to share in your last segment, you want to share it immediately to entice listeners to listen, or at least skip ahead to the part that affects them the most. Around this stage, you'll want to hear your intro jingle too. In the outro of your podcast script, you're going to want to make sure you're thanking all the guests who were on your show and recapturing a little bit of what's been talked of. This is also the right time to think about some exciting potential future shows and provide a call-to-action for the listener. You may want, for example, to support a special event that is important to your podcast and company, or to inspire listeners to become loyal subscribers.

2.2 Use of Content calendar to produce better Podcasts

If, at some point, you come up making efforts the day before your weekly (or whatever your release schedule looks like) publish date to come up with ideas for a podcast. So we'll talk in this chapter about how to set up a content calendar to streamline your podcast production process so that you get the most out of it. You might think that the advantages of having a content calendar are only in the categories of organization and time management, and it's right. There are huge gains to be had. But that's not the only way a well-designed content calendar can support your podcast, as we'll get to shortly.

Let's run through a benefits list.

- Reduce the uncertainty of publishing deadlines without revealing something
- Make your podcast releases more reliable. This is enormous to create the audience.
- Give yourself a reason to think about the content of your episodes in advance, and let ideas brew
- Have a system in place to break down your ideas and analyze them in better, more cohesive episodes
- Come off as a bad-ass podcaster getting your shit together and always becoming the envy of the podcasters.

Okay, so to begin with, we're not going to talk about preparation, scheduling, or any of that effects and materials that makes us feel like responsible adults contributing to society. Instead, we'll start by putting our spew on and dumping every idea we've ever had into a list for a podcast episode.

This section will be appealing to the public at large. Great content to support most is encouraged. News and current affairs related to the podcast theme are often of interest to a whole country. The subsequent reports can be more comprehensive and focus on particular areas of interest. Each section should be no more than 2-4 paragraphs, depending on the quality of the text.

In the podcast script intro, you can suggest introducing every episode of your podcast by this intro. Your listeners will listen to it a lot, so it is probably best to keep it short, maybe 10 or 15 seconds. With the +30 seconds skip setting on most podcast apps, the podcast intro won't be skipped over. What are you saying, then? Be sure to introduce the show host and its title. If you have any co-hosts, this is the right time to let your listeners know about them. Now is the time to give your viewers a glimpse of what they hope to hear on the show. For example, if you have something interesting and exciting to share in your last segment, you want to share it immediately to entice listeners to listen, or at least skip ahead to the part that affects them the most. Around this stage, you'll want to hear your intro jingle too. In the outro of your podcast script, you're going to want to make sure you're thanking all the guests who were on your show and recapturing a little bit of what's been talked of. This is also the right time to think about some exciting potential future shows and provide a call-to-action for the listener. You may want, for example, to support a special event that is important to your podcast and company, or to inspire listeners to become loyal subscribers.

2.2 Use of Content calendar to produce better Podcasts

If, at some point, you come up making efforts the day before your weekly (or whatever your release schedule looks like) publish date to come up with ideas for a podcast. So we'll talk in this chapter about how to set up a content calendar to streamline your podcast production process so that you get the most out of it. You might think that the advantages of having a content calendar are only in the categories of organization and time management, and it's right. There are huge gains to be had. But that's not the only way a well-designed content calendar can support your podcast, as we'll get to shortly.

Let's run through a benefits list.

- Reduce the uncertainty of publishing deadlines without revealing something
- Make your podcast releases more reliable. This is enormous to create the audience.
- Give yourself a reason to think about the content of your episodes in advance, and let ideas brew
- Have a system in place to break down your ideas and analyze them in better, more cohesive episodes
- Come off as a bad-ass podcaster getting your shit together and always becoming the envy of the podcasters.

Okay, so to begin with, we're not going to talk about preparation, scheduling, or any of that effects and materials that makes us feel like responsible adults contributing to society. Instead, we'll start by putting our spew on and dumping every idea we've ever had into a list for a podcast episode.

Excellent or mediocre, novel or cliché, laser-focused or amorphous blob that looks only barely like a concept at all, get them all out! Do not judge or categorize them at this stage; just take them out of your head and into a repository of some kind. When you have finished your brain dump, it's worth spending some time sorting the morass of ideas that are just sprawled like a mediocre burrito.

Some suggestions may include

- By how much the audience demands a subject
- Subcategories
- How happy you are with making an episode on the subject
- By how the content or structure of the episode is developed in your mind
- By the first color that comes to mind when reading the idea
- It is straightforward to underrate just how significant it can be to take the time to get the ideas out of your mind and organize them.
- It is time to move past the crayoning outside of this project's line phase and on to the scheduling. Again, when it comes to scheduling your shows, you have your range of devices to choose from. Confident choices include making a custom google calendar for your development schedule, putting it in Work Flow or your list app preference, or using any of the other infinite lists or scheduling software. You can also use whiteboards or cork boards if your person is an IRL type.

You will set up a system to keep your episodes scheduled for 4-6 weeks in the future but change the events weekly, filling out a little more details for each event as it gets closer to the date of recording. Your process could look like this:

- Six weeks out: Set the topic of the episode and set your intention. What would you want your audience to take away from this episode? Meet potential guests (if need be).
- Five Weeks out: List the points you wish to discuss in the episode. Confirm guests (if necessary) and start their studies.
- Four Weeks out: Come up with an episode structure and run with all the points and stories you want to tell. Come up with a list of guest interview questions (if necessary).
- Three Weeks out Episode record.
- Two Weeks out: edit the episode, build display notes, and get it ready to be published on your website and host.
- One week out: get your marketing posts prepared for the show, follow up with your guest (if you've had one) remind them of the release, and share how they can share them.

Keep in mind that each week you will do each of these tasks for this technique for a specific episode. Another choice would be to plan all 6 (or however many) adventures at once, following all the above measures at once, thereby giving you a "break" of six weeks before the next sprint. You can freely adapt and adapt to any of these systems to your workflow or something entirely new for you.

2.3 Podcast Equipment's needed for beginners

It is relatively straightforward to start a podcast, and you won't need much to get started. You can initiate with just a microphone, headphones, recording and editing tools, and a publishing site for sharing your work. You can get a bit fancier, of course, and chances are you may want to splurge on a couple of more significant ticket products as they can and do make life simpler, but that's all you need to get your show on the road. Podcast recording equipment can be puzzling to wade through and choose when to continue. You can get a lot of podcast gear, but that does not mean you require to buy it all – and you can always grow your podcast equipment list over time. We'll highlight the audio recording equipment you'll need, as well as some stuff you might want to do later as you get more serious about building a full podcast studio.

A computer and a microphone are the leading podcast equipment you will need in 2020, they are the first two products listed below. You'll want to avoid USB mics if you have several people recording together, which means you will also need an audio interface or mixer to connect up several XLR microphones. Again, look at the podcasting starter kit for more detailed suggestions for the equipment based on the number of posts you have. Beginners are given lower-budget options.

Computer

Access to Common Sense? To record and upload your .mp3 files, you need a computer. Most people are going to do just fine with what they've got, but if you're looking to upgrade, you should invest in something that's going to last you a couple of years.

Microphones

Audio is one place you do not want to cut corners in. With your podcast, the audience will be able to overlook a variety of problems — but lousy audio is widely known as unforgivable. You're going to skip the microphone that comes inside your device and then go for something like the Audio Technical ATR-2100-USB or Blue Microphones Yeti USB. You could also invest a little more and pick a dedicated XLR microphone — like the Samson SAC01 and a mixer, for improved quality and better sound performance. When selecting this option, don't forget to grab an XLR cable to attach the microphone to the blender. Don't use a built-in microphone on your computer. Using an usb microphone is the best way to get started. If you have multiple people or want more versatility, you'll need one or more XLR output microphones. Remember also your recording environment, and the type of microphone you want: dynamic or condenser.

Interface Audio

That is essentially the connection between your computer and your microphone. It transforms the microphone's analog signal into a digital signal which the device can use.

Mixer

The audio interface above is similar, but a mixer allows you greater control over speeds, inputs, outputs, and more. Especially important if you intend to have call-in guests regularly so you can set up a mix-minus line for remote guests.

Headphone

Headphones stop multiple errors and retakes. At first, it can be odd to hear yourself speak live, but you'll get used to it. It is strongly recommended that you get accustomed to this.

You don't want to record anything for an hour just to find that it wasn't switched on or that there was a loud buzz. Closed-back headphones are what you want to register, and perhaps your earbuds aren't good enough. Evite open-back recording headphones, as your microphone can pick up the sound.

Mount Shock

Microphones are especially sensitive to any sound not expected to pass through the air. A shock mount can avoid or mitigate intrusive noises from tapping the desk to typing to move your boom arm to tiny movements you cannot even hear. Even most microphone manufacturers sell a compatible shock mount, and some also include one with the microphone.

Cable Microphone

You need to plug your mic into an audio interface, a mixer, or somehow preamp. A lot is going into XLR microphone cables, and the cheap ones will cause more problems than they are worth.

2.4 Podcast Equipment for Advance Users

Several components go from content to systems and structure to making a podcast, but the podcast equipment is the central item without which you cannot produce anything. There is expensive equipment that gives control and quality to a recording studio standard, and then there are cheaper and less costly choices for those who just start and don't want to spend much. Once you start putting your podcast studio together, the first thing you can do is determine how much money you'll put into it.

That will depend on several factors. First, you should decide whether you're going to go podcasting as a casual hobby, or if you're going to want to expand and eventually make money.

Even you should know how much you're going to be podcasting, and what kind of quality you are seeking for and what you can afford. If you're looking for casual or not often podcasting, some of the starting and intermediate level equipment can help you get by.

However, if you take it seriously and believe it will impact your business, you recommend that you spend in higher quality equipment so you can produce the best quality podcasts. The best guidance is to get the bare essentials and consistently start doing podcasts if you're new to podcasting. When you gain some experience, you'll get a better idea of what you need and how to update your equipment as you go, but it's always easier to have the right systems in place so you can only focus on expanding and scaling. Do you want to enjoy podcasting and consider it worth it, but wouldn't you like to invest a lot in a better sound? You may be surprised to learn how a small price jump can make a big difference in quality. This device can be very costly, and a little more complicated, but if you put it in time, you can make it work well and hear the difference.

1. AT2020 XLR Microphone audio-technique

An inexpensive studio microphone, the AT2020 from Audio-Technica is a perfect option. It has a 20 to 20,000 Hz frequency response and provides excellent sound quality. The audio is vibrant and bright while the microphone handles high SPLs with ease. Note that it's not a USB mic, and there's no XLR cable to it.

2. Scarlett 2i2 Focusrite Studio Audio Interface Package

The Focusrite Scarlett 2i2 Studio Package is a set that includes Knox Gear Microphone Boom Scissor Arm with 5/8-27 Threading, Knox Gear Basic Microphone Shock Mount, and Knox Gear Pop Filter at an outstanding 4.6-star rating on Amazon, and included in Amazon's Pick.

It also comes with the software tools that allow you to plug in and start recording without trouble.

3. FiiO Q5s DAC Amplificator 768K/32Bit

This amplifier is certified for Apple MFi, Hi-Res Audio, and aptX, and supports encoding for Sony Walman players on iPhones, iPads, computers, and WM-PORT. It has interchangeable amp modules and plays with a crisp sound loud and clear. The amplifier comes with a USB Lightning-Micro cable, an optical adapter, a coaxial adapter, and a carrying case. It's a bit costly at just over $300, and it's sure to be an outstanding improvement to your old DAC / AMP.

4. Microphone with Pop Filter Shock Mount

This inexpensive pop-filter shock mount prevents microphone movement and vibrations when recording and changing the microphone angle. The pop-filter offers smooth audio. This shock mount comes with a universal connector adapter and is suitable for stereo and voice-over audio broadcasting.

5. Samson MBA38-38 "Boom Microphone Arm

Since the AT2020 microphone doesn't come with a microarm, Samsom Boom Arm is a good option for your studio equipment as an accessory. With a fixed clamp-grip of 3 inches, you can scale it up to 30 inches. It carries up to 5 pounds and is an incredibly inexpensive choice for intermediate podcasters at just under $80.

6. Shure SM7B Dynamic Cardioid Microphone

The Shure SM7B enters at $399 and is small and robust. This microphone boasts a smooth, wide-range frequency response and has excellent electromagnetic hum shielding. It also features 150 ohms connected to the receiver and is designed to reject off-axis audio in a cardioid pattern.

7. Sennheiser HD 650 Professional Headphones with open back

The Sennheiser HD 650 Open Back Headphones are designed specifically for accurate damping over the entire frequency spectrum. They that THD to an astonishing 0.05 percent and have an enhanced 10 39,500 Hz frequency response. They are lightweight and come with a cable of 118 inches. You will find them on Amazon at a discounted price of $369.93.

8. LiveTrak L-8 Podcast Mixer Zoom in

The LiveTrak zoom is suitable for professional podcasters and experienced audio mixers. This provides greater flexibility and options for tailoring audio rates precisely as you want them to. This 8-channel is primarily used for musical mixing but has everything you would ever need to apply for an audio podcast with a full range of pitch, boost, pan, and everything else adjustments. It's being sold for $399.99 on Amazon and has a 5-star rating of 4.5.

9. Samson MD5 Microphone Mobile Stand

The Samson MD5 Mic Stand measures 5 inches for advanced studio podcasting needs, and you can install your Shure SM7B mic on it. It features a weighted metal base to give maximum stability to the microphone and is equipped for keeping microphone and regular.

10. Cable 3 ft EBXYA XLR Microphone Cord

EBXYA XLR 3-feet microphone cords come in 10 different colors, so no trouble identifying which one is. These are suitable for DMX cables, stage cables, microphone cables, or instrument patch cables. For full insulation, they are covered with Oxygen-Free Copper (OFC) and Aluminum Foil.

11. Web Lifting Microphones

The Cloud Microphones Cloud lifter activator provides an inline boost of up to 25 dB of ultra-clean gain to your microphone. Besides, they charge the transformer of the microphones correctly for optimum performance. In other words, it will fix your rising audio issues for under $155.

12. Portable Recorder H6 Zoom in

Zoom H6 is a fantastic live podcast recorder. If you do not want to record using the amp on their machine, it comes in handy. It provides four simultaneous recording mic/line inputs and six songs. You will get it on Amazon for a reduced price.

Chapter 3: Tips for Podcast Recording and Editing

Home studio or office setups are great for podcast recording. With fewer distractions and better equipment, you have control over your surroundings, which you do not get while recording outside. Moreover, home recordings sound much more professional in a quiet area, with everything already set up and ready to use. However, there are better opportunities when taking your podcast on-site, for example, recording interviews on your phone adds to your shows a bit of variety and a new perspective. Record outside using iPhone's Voice Memos or Android's Voice Recorder to capture fascinating location-based conversations, then send them to your editing machine.

When you're making your podcast, you're probably a blogger, journalist, or subject matter expert with great ideas and stories but with a limited budget. Bad audio quality can distract from the message you're trying to convey, so having great-sounding, convincing audio is essential. Recording great audio takes some practice, but with these podcast recording tips, you can skip a lot of the trial-and-error. No amount of editing will make horrible source audio sound amazing, so use these to-the-point techniques to capture clean podcast recordings from start to finish. One of the final stages of the podcast creation process is editing the audio that you have recorded unless you do a live podcast. It may take a long time to write a podcast and can sound like a long job that prevents some people from moving from the documented to the published point. There are, however, methods that can help speed up the process and promote it.

3.1 Podcast Recording tips

1. Use the Proper Equipment

With your laptop's microphone, you can record a podcast, but we don't recommend it. To record professional and clear audio, you will need a few pieces of podcasting equipment. It is the best of all our podcast recording tricks, and it impacts the audio quality most.

2. Don't Forget to Stay Warm

To state the obvious, recording podcast episodes needs a bit of conversation. It is recommended 'warm up your mouth and vocal cords by practicing your script or saying a few tongue twisters, instead of going into your session cold'. This process of warming will 'improve your dictation'. It will reduce stumbling. There is nothing better than the first time you deliver your points flawlessly.

3. Record in a Tight, Comfortable Room

Record episodes to reduce noise and echoes from outside in the smallest and quietest place possible. Make sure to shut down your windows and doors, turn off any machines or appliances that make a constant noise, and put your pets somewhere they won't disturb you for a few hours. Using soft things (couches, pillows, curtains, etc.) to fill your recording space to absorb sound and muffle any errant noises.

4. Build a Short Profile of the Noise

During the beginning of the recording, pause for four to five seconds to build a noise profile. Stay silent and remove all noise from the environment. While recording, you can use this moment of silence to locate and delete any background noise by following The Audacity to Podcast's guide on noise reduction using Audacity.

5. Adopt Correct Strategies on Microphones

First, place your microphone at a height equal to your ears. Then sit back in a few inches and put the pop filter between your mouth and the microphone. First, concentrate on the distance of your mouth from the microphone system, and change your body to the volume level you want. Know, the closer you're to the mic, the louder the sound of your voice. You can settle the volume level of your voice during post-production to keep it consistent, when recording, raising your editing time by holding your mouth the same distance from the microphone.

6. Watch how much Volume you Have

You can track the volume rates while recording as you keep the microphone distance consistent. Most program recording shows the levels as a scale from green, yellow, to red. Hold the volume for the usual conversational tone and yellow parts in the green section when you need to put more emphasis. Stay out of the red section, or they will distort your sound.

7. Watch Out For your Breath

We all have to breathe, so managing your inhalation and exhalation sound will stop any significant wind gusts from creeping into your video. Stand up straight for smoother inhalations, consider taking smaller breaths, or push your mouth away from the mic when you breathe.

8. Hold the Flesh Still

Moving your body around during the recording creates background noise. If you use earbud headphones, this happens quite a lot. The wire lies across your face, causing your microphone to brush against your shirt and collar. Consider standing still with your feet planted in your chair. Evite the desk and switch stuff around. If you are printing your notes on paper, always pass them as quietly as possible

9. Remedy Hearing Issues Early

Record a test before you officially start plunging into your episode. If your guest's microphone has a problem or you can hear construction crew outside, don't try to push through. Identify and fix audio issues right from the start or even wait for the recording. The worst-case scenario is recording a complete episode only to discover out there is a bigger problem out you can't solve while editing.

10. Headphone Recording

While a podcast episode can be recorded without headphones, you'll usually get a lot of audio input from it. Having everyone with headphones will not waste your time in editing and cleaning.

11. Stand still while the Guests are talking

Simple sentences like "yeah" and "right" and "okay" are tempting to drop as your guests talk. These are natural language parts that we use without realizing that, but they can distract your listeners. Yes, during editing, you can remove them, but this is a lot of unnecessary work. Training yourself to restrict interjections is more straightforward, and allowing your guest or co-host to finish their thought.

12. Leave Audio Signs On for Errors

Mistakes also occur. They're not trapped in your episode forever because you're not making live performances. Slicing out mistakes is basic podcast editing, but to find them in the track, you have to give yourself a cue. Fortunately, there are various ways to do that. You can add a spoken marker where you say "delete the pizza restaurant story," then pause for a couple of seconds and continue. Find those pauses during editing, and remove the mistakes. Another choice, like a dog clicker, is a high-pitch sound marker that will create a spike in the volume. After the error occurs, press it a few times than note the peaks while editing.

13. Mute when you're Not Talking

By mutating your microphone while your co-host or guest is talking, save yourself some editing work. You won't pick up their speech in your microphone this way, and it's less noise you'll have to delete later on.

14. Use the Elements in Development Sparingly

Sound effects have a position to it. They can add life to your show and its uniqueness. But they may also confuse and cheapen using them too much. Only use sound effects when the content requires it, and stick to the results that suit your brand.

15. Just Stay Hydrated

Before you log, drink eight ounces of water or more. This will make your stomach relax, open your mouth, and help focus. It will also reduce any clicks of the mouth, the natural clicking and popping noises we make as dry as our mouth. Our stance is that drinking more water and pausing to use the bathroom once or twice is better than suffering the dehydration effects.

16. Log in a Separate Channel for Each Person

If you have multiple people in your show speaking, record each one on their site. This will allow you to control their volumes and noise profiles while editing. You can either tell people to record themselves on their computer (sometimes called a "double-ender") or use multi-track recording software.

17. The Record Under One Couverture

If you're trapped in a noisy environment, draping a blanket over you and your microphone is a simple way to reduce background noise. It's a gross strategy, but it is working. This is useful if you are forced to record in a busy hotel, car, or apartment building.

18. Don't Think About Pausing

Seek to split the series into segments with appropriate places to pause. It's always recommended to double-check the audio for any issues. Try to grab more water, and stretch your entire recording session to stay loose. Breaks are also excellent opportunities to talk to your co-host or guest about the next thing. You can schedule your chat, review notes, and even rehearse.

19. Maximize the Bandwidth on the Internet

If you are conducting an internet interview or chat, you must improve your communication as much as you can. That will boost the audio capture efficiency of your recording tools. How are you expanding your bandwidth? Besides switching to your internet provider plug it directly into your router (instead of connecting wirelessly) and close any program that does not use it. Ensure that your guests are instructed to sit in a place with a secure connection and also plug directly into their router, if possible.

20. Take note and trust your ears

The bottom line is trust in your heart, and do not think it over. Although initially just about everyone hates the sound of their voice, listening to everything that you record is essential. When you replay the audio files when something sounds off, follow your intuition. As you create more episodes and begin to like the final cut, take the recording setup notes and try to imitate it every time you get behind the mic.

3.2 Podcast Mixing Tips

Here's what you'd like to know right out of the bat: integrating vocals for podcasts is unique from blending choruses for music, where sheen, sparkle, luster, and other percussive adjectives are trendy to impart. Sure, you need to have your vocals on the podcast. Yet, most frequently, in a podcast voice aren't the main attraction — they're the only attraction. There is no context for them to rub against, no spiral synth or cymbal to sizzle. So when vocals are standing alone, you need to take specific steps to ensure the right sound.

1. De-essing

De-esing is the art of making sure your head is not torn off by sibilance. Keep in mind that the process is especially crucial for podcasts: people prefer to listen to episodes not on their HIFI devices, but on those small white earbuds that often make the upper-mid and high-end spectrum harsh. Therefore, it is best to use the principles discussed in this book, and to deploy them as drastically as possible without paying attention to the process; in other words, to keep it natural.

2. Pay Attention to your Changes

Be ruthless in editing, for the vocal will stand alone. You can choose to edit "ums," "ahs," and other out-of-the-box noises, but not too noticeable levels. You have to know from and never breach the rhythm of the human voice. First, look out for breath sounds, mouth clicks, lip smacks, plosives popping, and the like.

That's going to be easy to do because they're unnecessarily distracting. Lip smacks are done quickly: just mute their regions as long as they don't laugh in the middle of a word (or at the end of a breath). If they're embedded in a phrase, then you have choices. Technology to de-click will do the trick.

Or, if the smack is right, you can choose to slice the offending region back together and crossfade the results. That works occasionally; occasionally, it does not. Breath noises, especially those chopped off during editing, are another concern. There are plenty of plugins that promise results, but you can also cut breath noises by sight, isolate their regions, mutate them, and use a fade on the previous part. The same applies to plosives: in that case, the waveform will indicate where the plosives go out of control, slice out the offending waveform, leave the initial impact, and join with a subtle crossfade the remaining regions. Finesse takes a while, but it works more often than crossfading in the middle of terms for lip-smacks.

3. Learn how to Use Fades, Crossfades and Chamber Tones

Assure that their level correlates when bringing together two areas, and then massage the crossfades so that they are indistinguishable. It takes some rehearsal, but you will eventually get a feeling of crossfading two regions. Failure to do so will result in edits that sound obvious. Make sure you have some spare room-tone to loop underneath any moments of silence, for something has to replace the deleted lip-smack or neutralized breath, or the listener will hear the edit. Here's what you're doing: Place the room tone on a spare track, so it sits during the silent moment. For the fades, you will need audio on either side, as you may want to add one to the beginning of the zone, and another to the end. The listener does not note that the atmosphere is creeping in / falling out. If you are recording your podcast, be sure to mark the tone of the room here for use. It is not always possible, correctly, if you are mixing the project with someone else. In that case, catch any dead moment you might find — any delay, for example, between a question and an answer — and use that. When you need to string a few along, this will show you how to use crossfades.

4. Keep your Chain of Plugins Quick, but Successful

An EQ is one of the easiest and versatile tools available; it enables you to boost and cut various frequency ranges and bands. Some microphones are low-end dense, meaning you might want to use an EQ to reduce your low-end frequencies. Alternatively, some receivers are bright, which means you want the high-end rates to be lower. While applying boosts and cuts, using a reference track (ideally another high-quality podcast) to avoid tricking yourself into thinking that you are improving your audio when you do harm it in reality. The Scheps 73 EQ plugin is character-rich, and a best choice for adding that vintage warmth to the sound of your podcast. The Waves H-EQ Hybrid Equalizer is a thing to look at if you're looking for a bit more control and transparency. Using an EQ with a frequency analyzer to visually recognize the sounds you're concerned by. Then slim them down. For character, don't compress here; you're just attempting to control complexities — and lightly! Quite enough, compression and the apparent downloads pop, mouth sound effects, and sibilance increase. Not enough stabilization, and you're going to be spending more time modularizing concentrations than you would need otherwise.

5. Drop-offs Pick Up

When people put on their "broadcast voices," as they reach the end of a sentence, they tend to decrease in volume. Once you realize that drop-offs are inevitable, your editing work becomes much more manageable, as you know what a big part of it is. Clip-gaining the quiet parts up here is the game's nominal term, but be careful, it's a juggling act: you shouldn't lift the clip-gain to a point where the noise is noticeably louder. You should pursue a round of gradual processes, beginning with clip-gaining, going on to your plugin chain (where compression will carry down higher levels), and then move to volume automation.

6. Back to the Reduction of Noise

Noise-reduction is, without a doubt, the most misused tool in the podcasting game. It's the most significant harbinger of an unprofessional sound, and it's a frustrating process. At first, it all sounds good, but in the context of additional processing and hindsight, you begin to hear the noise reduction introduced by sonic problems. Which involve artificial ringing, a noticeable rise in sibilance, abnormal transient focus, and other obstructive noises. If that doesn't work, using the drop-off region subtly with sound, so that level boosts don't increase the overall atmosphere. But do not overdo this, since noising brings with it a host of problems.

7. Podcast Formatting for Streaming Services

Mastering is the process used to format podcast for streaming services. A tolerable amount of stereo bus compression may be in order if you have multiple people in your podcast. A prolonged attack (30ms) and short release (1-5ms) with a gain reduction of 1-2 dB will help pull all the voices you have recorded together and made them feel like they're in the same space. Bus compression is optional, and it may not be necessary; use your ears!

Since most podcasts contain speech primarily, there's not a lot to do when mastering your audio. If you come from a background in music production, you may be used to cut the lower end of vocals at around 80-100 Hz; this is not necessary for podcasts. For songs and music, the low end of the human voice conflicts with bass elements, but there is no bass element for it to clash with on podcasts. If you obliterate frequencies below 80-100 Hz, it will sound like something is missing.

If you are concerned about low-end rumble, you can still safely cut your track below 20-30 Hz without concern about losing your audio's vast body.

A loudness meter like the WLM Plus Loudness Meter will allow you to monitor your track's overall perceived loudness so you can make sure it sounds loud enough compared with other professional podcasts on the web. LUFS (loudness units relative to full scale) is used to describe differences in the loudness level over time, both in short and in the long term. Most streaming services apply a long-term LUFS-based gain reduction, so it's essential to know the long-term LUFS value of your podcast audio. Dynamic range affects the LUFS amount of your sound, so you can control the value of your music by applying more or less compression. The LUFS target for podcasts is -18 LUFS. This is slightly higher than the typical public radio LUFS target value, which is about -24 LUFS. Podcasts are often heard on mobile phone speakers and other hand devices. If the listeners are out in crowd and surrounded by noises, audio with a smaller dynamic range will be easier to listen to because of how it floats more effectively above the noise floor than sound with a higher dynamic range.

A limiter is a compressor that allows you to maximize the perceived loudness of a signal without clipping the audio. You set the level of your target output and compress your sound to the threshold you set. Limiters apply aggressive gain reduction, which prevents the incoming signal from exceeding the production you set. Setting your limiter output to 0dB is a poor choice. Although when you audition the audio file from your computer, it may sound fine. Once it is uploaded to streaming services, they tend to apply their formulas for reducing gain. If they see that the audio is too close to 0dB's digital loudness ceiling, they will use their gain reduction that may result in unwanted artifacts. Set your output level to no more than -1dB to avoid this; this prevents objects if the streaming service you upload reduces your audio level. Finally, export your audio to a bit depth of 24 and a sample rate of 44.1 kHz.

Also, make sure that you actively enable dither with noise shaping when exporting your audio; this adds low-level noise that can prevent the occurrence of audio artifacts. Once you have walked through this process a few times, recording future podcasts is relatively simple. If you register your podcasts each week, you will be able to save all the settings that work for you and call them the next week. With a bit of setup, and trial and error, you'll create all of your professional quality podcasts.

8. Apply Reducing Gain

You will note when recording your interview, that some parts will be noticeably louder than others. In old movies, you'll find that some parts are incredibly quiet, and others are extremely loud; raising higher and lower down the volume on your TV during a movie is a real fun-killer. New videos have gain reduction added to their audio, meaning you don't have to mess around with your TV volume; the sound is at a relatively constant level. Old films had a lot of dynamic variety, while new movies had a smaller dynamic range. The best way to implement gain reduction is to automate the gain level of the audio from your podcast inside your DAW; just bring it in. This is fine for a 1-minute segment, but there has to be a better way for an hour of the podcast, right? Yes, there are, of course! The solution is to add a compressor, a tool that reduces dynamic range. Waves Vocal Rider is a plugin that simulates someone using a mixing console to "rock" the fader. Vocal Rider automatically keeps the vocal and dialog levels steady, without drawing in any automation (although you can write the automatic riding to an automation track later). Riding a fader's input speed was an old trick that engineers employ to record outputs back in the day at a consistent level. Vocal Rider is excellent for attenuating your podcast's overall scale, but sometimes you'll need a bit more gain reduction, specifically for transient material.

You're going to want a compressor that can apply compression with a fast attack and release time; this will allow it to clamp down on transients, and quickly come back off when the audio falls below a certain threshold. The Waves Broadcast & Production Bundle contains many compressors suitable for transient compression, as well as a whole suite of other tools that will help improve the quality of the audio from your podcast.

3.3 Equipment Required to Edit Podcast

One of the most endearing qualities in podcasting is its accessibility. Not only can anyone make a podcast, but they should also all do a podcast. Editing a podcast means everything from tape cutting to mixing tracks to audio compression. And the software inside which you will do everything is a digital audio workstation (DAW). Your choice in software editing should first take a close look at your budget and objectives. Every DAW is different, and each serves a purpose that varies, sometimes wildly. But for everyone, there's a proper DAW out there.

Best Editing Software for Podcast

1. Pro Tools

Pro Tools is podcast editing software based on the Tesla Coupe DeVille. While it won't make you sound like a public radio program, the software that they're all using to package audio stories is more than probable. For some reason, Pro Tools is an industry-standard. It has every possible tool that you can imagine to record, edit, and master your audio. But all those bells (and all those whistles, too, while we're at it) come with a hefty price tag.

If you're just getting started, resist the urge to dive headfirst into the proverbial podcast waters using Pro Tools — unless you're ready for a steep learning curve. Once you have mastered the craft, however, you can use any DAW out there.

2. Adobe Talk

Adobe Audition comes with whatever you need. And if one thing's missing? On all the add-ons, you can tackle the content of your heart. But the real upside to Audition is the Adobe Suite — because it is all about the ecosystem, as Steve Jobs would say. If you turn out podcasts, there is a good chance that you will power that personal unicycle and spin your fair share of the plates. Your role probably involves a lot more than just editing. Knowing that Adobe can streamline your workflow as a whole. Let's talk through this — you master your final episode and have some outstanding clips in a social promotion that you want to feature. You can quickly grab those clips with Adobe, send them to After Effects to design an audiogram for your social, and get ready to send it out with Adobe Media Encoder. Given the Audition costs, it's probably the best option if you're already part of the larger Adobe Suite. If you're (and financially) a hobbyist at heart, Audition may be less of a priority.

3. Descript

Descript's evolution is worthy of note. What began as transcription software, Descript has grown into a podcast editing software with 'no experience necessary.' And the whole experience is rooted in word editing — not audio. You can record in Descript directly, or add a record later. Descript will spin a transcription, and the audio can be edited by editing the text.

Don't like a particular sentence? Delete it from the transcription, and select the audio track inside. There are a handful of other editing tools available for you.

The unique editing workflow may rob more experienced producers the wrong way, but starting a podcast is an easy way for beginners to do so. Also recently, Descript announced the new voice replication service Overdub that is powered by AI. Fun fact: HubSpot uses it.

4. Trickery

Audacity is just about more of an ethos than software editing these days. Yes, it does have all you need to start podcasting. Yes, that means tools that rival those you would find in costlier DAWs. Yes, it appears to have been designed during the waning days of 1998. But the best part of Audacity: Fully free (and open-source).

5. Band GarageBand

The mainstay of the Apple Music app Garage Band is mostly known for its digital instrument swath and music-making capabilities. GarageBand is an underserved software for podcast editing. Garage Band's convenience is simple: If you own a Mac, you own GarageBand. If you can use this to make and edit music, you can create and edit podcasts using it. You can quickly cut tape, move audio sections around, and layer in sound all in that user-friendly classic Apple experience. GarageBand is an excellent option for people who already own Apple products, are new to editing, and want to learn the basics of what podcast editing software offers.

3.4 Ways to Edit Podcast

In addition to creating the content itself, podcast editing is arguably the most critical step in producing a podcast that your subscribers would like to hear. The ubiquity of Digital Audio Workstations (DAWs) and other editing software makes the editing power easily accessible. Still, it can be challenging to know where to start if you're not an audio professional.

Things to consider before editing

1. Remember Publishing is where your Story Takes Place

In the service of your content, the technical & tactical should always be used. It's easy to get lost in the weeds once you start the editing process, so make sure you know what you're trying to accomplish before you put the finger on your audio. Before you start, listen to your recording, take notes, and decide what's important to you and your listeners. Decide what you're editing at the outset and why and you're going to stay out of time-wasting rabbit holes.

2. Small Planning Goes a Long Way

Decisions made during the pre-production and recording stages of your podcast episodes can simplify your editing considerably. Experience is the best teacher here, but there are plenty of available resources, such as writing the right interview questions or using proper microphone techniques to prevent headaches in your editing. Learn and apply one new technique/concept per episode, or select a handful per season, and watch exponentially develop your expertise. Here are three ways to better organize your podcast editing workflow:

1. Use consistent folder structure and conventions on filenames. When you produce volume content, standardization is your best friend-don't leave yourself wondering where you're putting that clip. Choose a system that works and stick with you.

2. Use dedicated tracks for various audio in your DAW-voice-over, dialog, field recordings, sound effects, music, and ads, and group them by example. You may be tempted to use fewer tracks to keep everything immediately visible on the screen, but don't.

It is a messy approach that will lead to a complicated, sloppy mix. Session organization is a pro audio move that you can implement right now, regardless of the level of skill, and it will set you up well for mixing and creating templates.

3. Separate tasks to edit content and to edit sound. If your interviews are extended, get them transcribed with timestamps, and create a punch list of transcription content edits. Listen for any audible distractions you may need to address and then tackle those once the content edits are done.

Whatever your software choice is, most will share a standard set of features, including different toolbars, a transportation section (stop/play/record, etc.), a workspace or timeline where you can add audio clips/regions to tracks, and a built-in audio editor for some DAWs such as Garage band.

Technique 1: Workflow Based on the Track

Suppose you just opened a new session in your DAW. In nearly any application, you should be able to select files to be imported in the menu bar via "File > Import," or simply select them on your computer and drag them into the (Digital Audio Workstations) DAW workspace. Most DAW's also have built-in keyboard shortcuts. These vary by app, but once you learn them, you can dramatically speed up your work. Many DAWs will automatically sort audio clips onto their tracks upon import, but if yours doesn't, create a new record for each clip and add it from the audio bin of your DAW. A track-based workflow has the main advantage of independent control over each audio clip in your session. Clip cuts and fades, the ability to move clips forward / backward in time, the processing of plugins, the volume levels, the panning, and the automation of these parameters are all track-specific choices that will help you create the episode you want to hear – more in the future.

Technique 2: Build a Punch List

Once you have imported your tracks and sorted, it is time to start editing. If you have gone down the annotated transcript route, begin running the punch list down. You may want to either listen to your raw recording and editing in real-time or B listen to your disk or create a punch list of edits if you haven't created one yet. This can be a useful way to collaborate on the edit and stay on the same page if you are working on a team.

Technique 3: Tools, and a Workflow Based on Clips

Most DAWs include a comparable tool/feature suite including select, trim, grab, cut/split, and fade. In short, here's what the tools are, and when to use them:

- Select-works in your word processor of choice similar to a cursor to select one or multiple clips.
- Trim-allows the shortening of an audio clip by simply dragging in from the edge and revealing previously trimmed audio.
- Grab-allows you to grab and move the entire clip forward or backward in time, or drag it on to another track.
- Cut / split-separates your clip by creating a sub-clip of the source file at a given point of your choice.
- Fade-comes in three iterations: fade in, fade out, and crossfade through. A crossfade is just a combination of the other two, one clip fading in at the same time as the other one fades in. The use of a fade in / out at the edge of an isolated cut or a crossfade between adjacent clips mitigates any potential pops or clicks that may result from a wound.

Technique 4: Make Edits

The most straightforward approach for content edits is to make and delete a pair of cuts at the boundary of unneeded audio. Then use the grab tool to drag and close the gap on a resulting couple of clips, applying a crossfade between the two new clips at the joint. If the beginning or end of a clip is to be trimmed, use the trim tool to drag the edge of the clip to your desired timing and add a fade in or fade out as needed. Follow the same logic for sound edits when an audible distraction occurs within a recording gap.

Chapter 4: Marketing of a Podcast

You are in the right place if you want to learn how to advertise a podcast and develop a listenership. You probably got into podcasting to spark a conversation around a topic about which you are passionate. Cultivate a community of listeners from around the globe who share your interests, who appreciate your views on a subject. Let's take one step back to assess our podcast foundation before we jump right into our top promotional strategies. We will start with the two main pillars of podcasting, the content of quality, and the time. We need to make sure that what we are creating right now is worth promoting, and we have realistic expectations about the timelines of success. Marketing a lousy product is time-waste. No money of any quantum, creative marketing angles, or strategies from Hail Mary will make a stale podcast grow. First, make sure it's up to snuff before you start trying to crack the code on promoting a show.

What is it that makes a good product? Those three qualities have to be hit:

- Valuable: There is something for your listeners to gain from the episode. Either they learned new information or skill, were entertained, or curiosity was satisfied.

- Unique: Your podcast's point of view podcast adds something new, albeit slight, to the conversation. Uniqueness for each topic varies, so start with creating Venn Diagrams in your niche against others. Focus on refining your differentiating factors first when too many data points to land in the middle.

- Sticky: You need podcast to capture and sustain the attention of an audience. If your current listeners don't consume your episodes in full consistently, better focus your efforts on the content. Listen to podcasts similar to yours, study their formats, their content, and their structure. Consider how you can incorporate those features into your show and improve on what they've created.

- Providing value is the best long term strategy for promoting a podcast. In the short term, gimmicks and shortcuts may work, but they won't support you. Rather than leaping to the latest marketing trend, focus on value creation through strong relationships and quality content.
- With quality content beneath your belt, turn next to the second important pillar: time. We know that Rome wasn't built in one day, and we can say the same for podcast audiences. Remember, many hosts produce a 5-6 month podcast before seeing significant upticks in their listenership. That means promoting ten top-notch episodes that see minimal engagement in the end. Don't be deterred. Faith that developing a podcast takes time and growth depends on producing consistently engaging content.

4.1 How to Launch and monetize podcast?

Here are few strategies to explore for direct podcast monetization. Choose the ones which fit your show best.

1. Request Contributions

The easiest way of monetizing a podcast is by asking people for money. Many fans are happy to throw a couple of dollars at their favorite podcasters to make sure they keep getting great content. You can add a PayPal button to your site, or open a Stripe account, and add a donation form. Or set up a GoFundMe activity for a simple collection page. Keep your calls-to-action authentic to avoid feeling slim about this kind of self-promotion.

Are you asking for donations to create new episodes so you can spend more time? Tell the audience. If people understand where the money goes, they will be more apt to donate.

2. Create Paid Third Party Membership

Podcasting's latest trend is to create paid membership tiers. Listeners can pay to access exclusive content, Facebook private groups, or podcast swags. The best way to start that is by creating a Patreon account. It is well-respected and user friendly. You can use their automatic settings, or create your donor level and reward system. If you're going with Patreon, play around with the options for leveling. Fans can be rewarded with swag, content, or other perks for their contributions. You may find more listeners willing to support the show because, for their participation, they receive either a physical product or exclusive episodes.

3. Sell Patronage or Ads

The most usual way of monetizing a podcast is through sponsorship. It's also the easiest aside from accepting donations because you don't have to create or sell anything. You just need to settle a sponsor deal. You've probably heard podcasters begin their show or break in with something like, "The [some company] is bringing this episode to you. If you're looking for a ... "then you get that idea. It is a sponsorship. Sponsorships pay more, based upon how many people are listening to your show. As the number of people listening increases, so will your earnings. But that also means that if you don't have a lot of listeners, this is a tough way to make money. You can generally charge the mentions for "pre-roll" and "mid-roll." Mid-row (they pay more during your episode). If you are comfortable, promote the sponsor at both points.

4. Join a Publicity Network

Advertising networks such as Advertise Cast, Midroll, Popcorn, and Pod Grid act as intermediaries between sponsors and hosts. They will take a cut from the advertisement placements included in your show when applying for each platform, so be sure to read the fine print. The revenue share typically follows a CPM model where you are paid for every 1,000 impressions served by the ad unit. Disturbed? This is what the maths boils down to. Advertise Cast has a 70/30 revenue share model in which the podcast host receives 70% of the revenue earned and 30%. If a podcast has gathered between 1,000-2,499 listeners per episode, the ad unit of 30 seconds has a CPM of $23. The sponsor pays $46 after 2.000 listens. That's $23 * 2 because per 1,000 listens, the sponsor is charged. The podcast host is ultimately taking home $32.20, and Advertise Cast is taking $13.80. It's crucial to estimate what you might earn from a publicity network, depending on your reach. Advertise Cast has a calculator for pricing, which determines the total cost of ad units placed in your show. Just remember, only 70 percent of the total will be taken home.

5. Sell Episodes Premium

Because you know that your audience likes to listen to your podcast, some of them are likely to pay for premium versions of your content. All you need to do is create some exclusive recordings which are available for purchase only. A simple way of creating premium content is to record it while recording your free stuff.

Let's say you're inviting a guest to their show. Record a discussion lasting 30 minutes, then add another 10 minutes to sell as a bonus. Make sure that there is something juicy people will want to buy for 10 minutes extra.

A word of warning here: make sure that there is still a lot of value in your free stuff. You don't want your listeners to assume that you hide all the good things in the paid content, or that they won't bother.

6. Gate your Catalog to the Back

If you started a podcast age ago and built up a catalog of episodes from behind, try this strategy. You can limit access to your older events instead of creating new Premium content. This means you will be adding a paywall to listen to the older material for users.

7. Sell Repurposed Material

A great way to create sealable content is to repurpose things that you have created before. This shortens the time you'd spend doing something similar. Take some of your best podcast episodes that touch on related topics. Transcribe them yourself or use automatic transcription services directly from your dashboard to Castos. Then edit the recordings, add more value and resources wherever you can, and pack them into a book. If your listeners appeal to this strategy of monetizing a podcast, invest a little money in a professional design. You can then put it in a format that suits Amazon. Selling Amazon's books is far more effective than trying to sell it over your website. Next, market your new Podcast book. Point out that all you've taught is a comprehensive way to learn.

8. Log in your YouTube Show

An easy way to squeeze out some cash from what you've already created is to publish your podcasts as videos on YouTube. This process is swift. All you are supposed to do is enable monetization in your account settings, and Google will handle the ads and distribute the money. You are not required to do much editing of the video. Just add a single image to your recording of the episode.

Also, think of best practices in YouTube SEO to surface your videos in more search results. How much do you do on YouTube? It depends on several factors, such as how long people watch video views, whether they skip your ads and whether they click on your ads. You can earn between $0.50 and $2.00 per view, in general.

Here are even more ways to make your podcast money. Check out some of those techniques to indirectly monetize a podcast.

1. Selling Physical Goods

If an audience loves a podcast, they could buy merchandise showing in the show. You could sell t-shirts, mugs, stickers, or anything that allows your audience to connect outside listening to the latest episodes. Show the name of the podcast, a repeated phrase about the catch, or an inside joke on the merch. Your calls-to-action can depict the moment a listener may pass a stranger on the street and realize that their favorite show is wearing a tee-shirt. A bond is formed instantly out of their shared love for your presentation. And these days, to have your e-commerce store, you don't have to handle any products. You can design and showcase products with Teespring, which are only printed/created when someone purchases them. You don't have to put down any money in that way. With Oberlo, when your customers place an order, you can create a drop-shipping store that automatically purchases products from another source.

2. Speaking in Public

For a lot of podcast hosts, public speaking is a simple transition. If you talk on your show comfortably, you're likely going to do well in front of a crowd. To be sure, standing before a bunch of people is a unique challenge, but if you already know how to craft a script, it is less of a problem. How much of a speaking fee you can make varies widely.

Some speakers are getting a small amount of stipend and travel costs. Others make six or more figures. How do you get to speak in public? Find local groups meeting to talk about your niche or industry. Try to source the Meetup, Facebook groups, or even your local paper that organizes the event. Contact them and offer them a topic to present but be open to their topic ideas. Let them know you plan on plugging your podcast. Prepare a Visuals presentation and outline a script. Initially, you'll have to start small. Don't expect stadiums to fill up – or even auditoriums. 5-8 people will attend your first speaking gigs, but that's all right. Use these gigs to fine-tune your presentation skills and make relations.

3. Sell Slots for the Mastermind

A mastermind group is a unique way of monetizing a podcast because it gives you more value than just money. A mastermind is a group of few people who are dedicated to supporting each other towards a common objective. They provide education, brainstorming, and accountability to help you keep track of what you're trying to learn. You are also a member of a mastermind group, which means you have to limit it to a small group of people, which can also add value to your business. You shouldn't be a teacher, but because you're the organizer, you can still charge for slots. However, the challenge with masterminds is that members expect value. They place a tremendous amount of work into it, too, so they won't be satisfied if you or anyone else that is part of the mastermind disappears for a week or two. If you choose to promote your podcast on this avenue, you need to commit to it. If your members are close, you can meet in person, but online masterminds work well too. We endorse using a private group, like a working space on Facebook or Slack.

4. Sell e-course Access

If your podcast is educational or aims at teaching a new skill to listeners, creating a stand-alone e-course is the perfect way to make money. You can either create a course on your website (with a tool such as Member Press) or host it on a third-party platform such as Udemy, Coursera, or Skillshare. If you think that courses are the right way to monetize a podcast, we recommend that you create your first course on one of those third-party platforms. Yes, you're going to pay some fees for each person taking the course, but you're going to skip building a functional system on your website. If it turns out that courses are your money-maker, then bring it all in-house.

5. Sell Upgrades to Contents

Including a downloadable resource with each podcast episode related to that episode is smart to monetize a podcast. This is called upgrading material because it upgrades or enhances listener experience. Let's say you're hosting a podcast on fishing, for example. In one episode, you are talking about trout fishing. You ask your fans to go to your website at the end of the episode and buy your 99-part map of the best U.S. trout fishing spots. To sell a content upgrade, you will need to place a payment form somewhere on your site for listeners to pay for and download it. The most feasible place for this is the page where you publish the links and audio player to download your podcast. And if you sell upgrades of content to monetize a podcast, you can also add an e-commerce shopping cart to your site so that you can list your upgrades of content individually. This way, people will be able to browse your previous upgrades in one place instead of sorting through every post.

6. Sell Product Information

Information about the product is a kind of content that people buy to learn new things. A template, a material, a guide, an eBook, a worksheet, etc. could be anything. A general information product, unlike content upgrades, does not have to relate to a specific episode, but would solve a broader issue or problem that your listeners face. The most significant advantage of selling information products through your podcast is that you can plug them in your podcast script as often as you like so that sales do not fall flat. You can also give your listeners questions or comments, and answer them on your show, which adds more value to your purchase.

7. Sell your App

A podcast can be monetized if you acutely know of the challenges and problems facing your listeners by designing an app that suits their needs. If you are hosting a parenting podcast, you could be selling a calendar app specifically designed for parents. If you are hosting a podcast on astronomy, you might be selling a star-finder app. Alternatively, you may be selling a simple branded app that will help people interact better with you and your content. It could have episodes of your podcast, blog content, updates, schedule, and perhaps a way to speak directly to you.

8. Hosting an Event

Sell away the tickets to a live event where your followers can meet you in person if you have a local follower or a devoted audience who wouldn't mind traveling to see you. The kind of occasion that you are hosting will depend on your audience and the subject of your podcast. You could give a lecture, run a workshop, teach a skill, or simply host a group discussion. Eventbrite is an excellent tool for selling your tickets to a live event.

That's a challenging way to monetize a podcast, to be fair. We recommend that you stick to this tactic until you have a faithful following. Events don't need thousands of people to turn a profit, but some people are needed to show up. And if you are considering hosting events on traveling to new cities, analyze where your listeners are first. Head to the analytics dashboard of your podcast host, and go through the geographic reports. A no-brainer is organizing events in cities where you already have one.

9. Sell Consultancy Services or Coaching Services

The most significant advantage of hosting a podcast is that you are establishing yourself in a niche as an authority. As an informed expert, your audience comes to respect you. A great way to make money out of a podcast is to provide services that relate to your subject. A productivity and wellness podcast, for example, could offer personal life coaching. A marketing podcast could sell personalized marketing strategies. Starting here is relatively easy. You just need a landing page with a form or widget on your web site for people to sign up for a coaching session. What is a Session of Coaching? They can be whatever you like. It could be as easy as a phone call or chat with Skype, or as complex as a visit in person at the client's location. Put together any type of service that's right for your client.

10. Sell Products to Affiliates

Some firms have open affiliate programs that you can take advantage of. You don't need to settle a deal or get approved. Simply sign up and tell them where to send out your payments. Whenever someone signs up with your link, you get paid. Instead of creating your products for sale, you might be able to sell products from other people for a cut in sales. There are two ways of doing that.

The first method is to self-promote their products. Audible's partner program, for example, is common among podcasters. They give you a free promotional link. Using your link, you get $15 every time someone signs up for a free trial.

11. Generate Leads in Business

Many companies start podcasts to support bigger initiatives. Fast Company found even back in 2018 that "branded podcasts are the ads people want to listen to." If you are hosting a podcast that complements your business, you are in the perfect position to generate highly qualified leads. Say you own an accounting company, for example, and recently started a podcast that educates people about how to make their taxes. While you're giving away free suggestions on the show, you're also weaving the value of doing the taxes of people for them in your company. When April comes around, who is your listeners' first company to think about managing their complicated tax returns?

4.2 Strategies to Promote your Podcast

You are in the right place if you want to learn how to promote a podcast and grow a listenership. You probably got into podcasting intending to spark a conversation around a topic about which you are passionate. Cultivate a community of listeners from around the world who share your interests, who appreciate your views on a subject. There's a process to figure out exactly which tactics are right for your show, with so many marketing strategies to choose from. Keep those two factors in mind as you work to find your perfect marketing mix.

Focus on the Audiences

It is great if people like your podcast, but it probably isn't.

Rather than marketing all podcast listeners, focus on those who get the most benefit from your show. Take steps over time to learn about that audience as much as you can, so you can design promotions that will find them with the right message. Incorporate everything you know about your listener into a persona document so that you can refer to it when creating marketing copies.

Test and Measure

It's essential to try new things and measure their results whenever you take steps to promote a podcast. You should run several tests to find the tactics that work. Let's assume you decide to answer questions on Quora, for example, to get traffic to your podcast website. In your answer, it would be smart to add tracking codes to the links to know how many people end up landing back on your site. Without any tracking parameters, it's hard to decide whether or not a tactic is successful. The data generated through experiment tracking provides actionable insights into what channels are driving new subscribers. In marketing, it's a better strategy to focus on the real world numbers than to go with your gut feeling.

Podcast promotion is not a game of one-size-fits-all. For one show, a strategy that floods hundreds of downloads can be a slow drip for another. Keep in mind variety when charting a marketing strategy, and see what sticks. In the beginning, you'll need to go through trial and error, estimating what works and on which channels. Testing new ideas, various messaging angles, and pushing yourself out of the box may uncover the audience you've been looking for.

1. Release Three Episodes at Least on the Day of Launch

If you haven't started your podcast yet, before you release, create at least three episodes. If you don't have a couple of episodes to explore for new listeners, there's a good chance they won't get invested and probably will forget you.

2. Submit Aggregators and Directories on Podcast

A podcast aggregator is an app that plays podcasts, called a podcatcher. Apple Podcasts, the automatic podcast app that comes with iOS, is the most well-known podcatcher. But there's a lot more to come, including Google Play, Spotify, TuneIn, and iHeartRadio, Sound Cloud, Pod bay, and Pod tail. Set up accounts and submit your RSS feed to each podcast directory so that new episodes will be published automatically on each medium. This will reveal you to new audiences as they navigate their preferred listening app to consume new shows.

3. Prompt your Listeners to Sign Up, Share and Leave their Reviews

At the start and end of each episode, ask your listeners to subscribe, share, and review your podcast. The best way to place that calls-to-action is to be authentic rather than pushy. Be honest and explain that you'll be able to produce better content for your audience to enjoy as your podcast grows.

4. Published During Strategic Times

When we discussed how to promote a podcast with one of our customers, he said you must publish it at strategic times. Look at similar podcasts if you are just starting and identify when they are posting. If you see a trend, there is probably a reason for that. Follow that trend until you have data of your own. Grave through your podcast analytics over time to see when people are listening to your episode. Experiment to see if it's true if you see a trend within your audience.

5. Don't Forget the Rear Catalog

Your back catalog is full of exciting content and the perfect way to get new subscribers hooked on. If you mention a topic that you covered in a previous episode, add a quick aside with the episode number: "If you want to learn more about productivity, check out episode # 17 where we talked to John about managing a busy schedule." Recall linking to them in the show notes to make it easy for the listener to find out.

6. Taking Advice from the Word of Mouth

Word of - mouth advertising is one of the most effective possible marketing strategies. Step one is to find the right places to spread your message. Your audience is gathering in the real world in certain situations, so it's your job to find them and also to attend. Research conferences, meetings, or local events related to your podcast, in your area. Then, when you go, have a plan to make the most of the event beforehand. Inter-connect your heart out by talking to the participants and speakers of the event. Do not be afraid to mention that you are working on a podcast and how it relates to your attendance.

7. Podcasters Network with Other

To promote a good podcast means to remain on top of new ideas, trends, and techniques. Joining a community of other podcasters is the best way to keep yourself informed. They'll help you, provide support, and discuss new ways to promote your podcasts. If you fully invest in a community, that can become one of your best resources.

8. Foster Relevant Podcasts across Borders

Other podcasters are likely to have similar audiences to yours. Reach those creators and ask for a cross-promotion to be set up. Simple: you're talking about them, and they're talking about you. Begin by reaching out to audiences of the same size as yours. Most likely, they will respond.

9. Be a Guest, and Call a Guest

Pitching yourself on another show as a guest is a great way to present your content to an aligned, qualified audience. Similarly, it produces more engaging episodes, including interesting guests on your show, and adds a unique perspective for your listeners. Be sure to create a podcast press kit that allows guests to share the episode easily. Focus on working with other niche podcasts and have a complementary audience to yours.

10. Get in Touch with People you mentioned on your Show

If you mention a person or brand in your show, reach out to them after the episode has been published. Remove the quote you spoke about their product and ask if they would be willing to share your show on social media. This usually only works if anything that you have said has been positive. When we asked some of the hosts, we were working on promoting a podcast without investing a lot of time; this was standard advice.

11. Value-Added for Online Communities

There are likely to be millions of conversations about your podcast topic on Facebook, Quora, Reddit, and Twitter. One of your episodes might add value to the discussion, and introduce new listeners to the show. Search each platform for threads and forums related to your show. Once you find a few groups that are committed enough, start adding your value. But be vigilant. That strategy is wise. Focus first on being just part of the conversation without promoting your show. It will be beneficial to be part of the community when the right post to promote yourself comes along.

Conclusion

Podcasts are more comfortable than blogging posts; people can hear to podcasts while driving, working out, or doing house chores. Podcasts are as diverse as the people that make them. History, pop culture, psychology, and even a fantasy city where aliens are buddies with the Yeti are great podcasts. The only obstacle to producing a podcast is your creativity. There is substantial unexplored space in the podcasting industry. Apple Podcasts include at least 600 million forums, 23 million YouTube channels but just 800,000 podcasts. You do not need to be a technical guy, nor do you need any money to learn how to do a podcast.

If you understand the importance of producing content for your company and brand (e.g., blogging), you know the value of podcasting. A good podcast, like any good piece of material, should address the audience's needs: a difficulty or issue to be solved, a question they need to answer, or a subject they want to learn more about. Determining how frequently your podcast (their frequency) depends very much on your content. If you're talking about a weekly television show, then it's quite apparent you should have a weekly podcast. Your frequency dramatically depends on the length of each episode. When you have an incredibly loyal audience, it seems overkill to release one-hour episodes every day (under the same podcast that is).

If a customer goes on a one-week break, they must return to five hours of the content of that series, which can be quite challenging.

But a monthly podcast on the opposite side should not automatically be a two- or four-hour show. Research all components of your podcast to provide your audience with the most relevant material.

Your writing style should be conversational with a friendly language, restricting the use of jargon or industry-specific terms to please your listeners. The first segment will be the most interesting for holding the attention of listeners. This section will be appealing to the public at large. Great content to support most is encouraged. Podcasting's latest trend is to create paid membership tiers. Listeners can pay to access exclusive content, Facebook private groups, or podcast swags. The best way to start that is by creating a Patreon account. The most usual way of monetizing a podcast is through sponsorship. It's also the easiest aside from accepting donations because you don't have to create or sell anything. You just need to settle a sponsor deal.

www.ingramcontent.com/pod-product-compliance
Lightning Source LLC
Chambersburg PA
CBHW051538240526
45465CB00027B/684